What Career Should I Choose?

What Career Should I Choose?

RABBIT

Copyright © 2012 by RABBIT.

Library of Congress Control Number: 2012901264
ISBN: Hardcover   978-1-4653-9635-8
              Softcover   978-1-4653-9634-1
              Ebook   978-1-4653-0601-2

All rights reserved. No part of this book may be reproduced or transmitted in any form or by any means, electronic or mechanical, including photocopying, recording, or by any information storage and retrieval system, without permission in writing from the copyright owner.

To order additional copies of this book, contact:
Xlibris Corporation
1-800-618-969
www.Xlibris.com.au
Orders@Xlibris.com.au

Contents

1. The Starting Block 1
2. Stages of Life 4
3. Commitment 7
4. Some Questions to Define What the Future May Look Like 9
5. A Little Bit of Explanation 12
6. Questions About Yourself 15
7. What Are Your Likes and Dislikes? 17
8. What Would You Like to Achieve? 19
9. When Do You Think You Will Retire? 24

PART 2—The Four-step Schedule 27

Foreword

Hi, there.

I am so pleased to meet you.

Yes, I know where you have come from.

By now you are in year ten of high school or maybe year eleven or twelve, and there isn't much time before you graduate and go out into the real world, leaving school behind.

CONGRATULATIONS

That indicates that you have achieved a lot in the years that you have been attending school. Many of you:

1. *Can* count, and more than likely, know your times tables.
2. *Can* spell words and are very familiar with the alphabet.
3. *Are* physically active and play sport.
4. Have parents or significant adults in your lives, and you, more than likely, have siblings.

5. Probably have friendly rivalry between you and your siblings.

However, on to the crux of the matter.

What Career Should I Choose?

Throughout the following pages, you will gain insight and depth of knowledge as to how to ascertain actually what you need to accomplish, including the four steps to have a successful career.

So let's get started!

This will take between six and eighteen months to complete, depending upon the level of intensity you use in completing the requirements as defined within the four-step schedule.

PS: If you have already left school and need a career change, this will also suit you. Just work through the four-step schedule after having read all of the preceding chapters.

# The Starting Block

In the beginning, yeah, well, moving right along . . .

You want to know what career you should choose.

To say that it is simple and easy would do the required analysis an understatement.

On the attached four-step schedule, there are a number of questions which you are required to answer at different time intervals. But to start with, it is highly suggested that you read every page of this book before moving on to the schedule.

The four-step schedule helps you to proceed in a systematic manner along a logical pathway to be able to, from your true responses to the questions posed, lead you to being able to realise what career best suits you and how to access it.

Whilst school has been a place to attend for the past few years, and the knowledge gained sits in layers in your mind, the knowledge that you are using is the theory that you have gained throughout your school life. The real work starts when you use that knowledge in a practical manner and the knowledge then becomes your interpretation of the learnt theory for whatever purpose in your life you are applying it to.

I could give many examples, but let's just take the colour red: it is in your sight a colour of brightness or can represent a stop sign or a stop light as in traffic lights or the colour of a football jersey and has many hues rather than just being a stand-alone colour, and it branches out into a multitude of shades and various forms whilst still being the basic red colour.

All colours throughout the rainbow have multiple uses; the colour blue is not only the colour of the ocean but also the colour of a bruise as well as many other things.

This booklet sets out to encourage you to use your mind in such a way that it encourages you to think about yourself, your strengths, your weaknesses, your opportunities, and of course, finally threats against your own success.

It is a very good starting point to put this book down and, in your own manner, answer the following questions:

This is a *SWOT analysis*, and the following questions need to be answered:

What Career Should I Choose?

1. What are your strengths?
2. What are your weaknesses?
3. What are your opportunities?
4. What are the threats or obstacles?

In your own time, you should answer each of the above questions. Repeat the exercise after six and twelve months later. But you will find the above in the results book at the end of these chapters together with examples befitting to each of the questions.

Following on from that, there are many little questions which will direct you towards the area which will best suit you, your personality, and your short-term goals and lead you upon the right path for your ultimate long-term goals.

Questions like:

> Do you like being inside or outside in the fresh air all day?
> Do you want to wear a uniform like a policeman or a member of the armed forces?
> Are you inspired enough to teach students?
> Would working in the medical field be of interest to you?
> Do you want to be a journalist?
> Does a profession inspire you, e.g. being an accountant or an architect, to name a few?
> Do you want to work with your hands?

2 Stages of Life

A short interlude here to briefly describe the stages you can expect to experience in life:

Age 0–8 years — From your birth through the very first years of education. By the time a child has achieved the age of eight, he/she is able to tell the difference between right and wrong, is able to do a lot of things for themselves, by themselves, and is able to express themselves, both verbally and in written form. There is still the requirement for parental control and parental involvement.

Age 8–12 years — A child is able to participate in sports, be competitive, be a team player, be a willing member of a group, be it a family group or a classroom of students, and be able to see the importance that they play within their own world.

What Career Should I Choose?

Age 13–20 years	Now the hormones start to show themselves with physical development becoming obvious. Growth spurts coupled with the awkwardness of the teenage years make this a complex time but one which is paramount to the maturing process. Then there are the educational requirements which will lead to graduating from high school and then furthering the education at either an university or, for some, a college course or a Technical and Further Education (TAFE) field of endeavour or an apprenticeship.

Age 20–30	This is when people finalise education, strengthen social contacts, find a partner, work hard, diligently climb the ladder of employment, and increase their income, start to purchase property, take on a mortgage, become more mature, create realistic plans for the future, and even maybe start their own family.

Age 30–50 years	At this stage, you become your own person, are still a team player both in sports and at work, pay your mortgage off and become debt free, educate your children to see that they achieve a very high standard of education and teach your children how to be good parents by being an exceptional parent yourself. Now that parental responsibilities have lessened, it is a good time to start an interest or a hobby with your partner. This could be anything; stamp collecting, share investment, anything that creates a joint interest in an area which is different to your usual combined points of interest. Be aware that your brothers, sisters, and parents will still require time with you. Prepare to build your asset value – the choice of how to is up to you and the questions that you ask and the people that you speak with and associate with will all help you to formulate your plan and ideals and probably help you to strive for more and be able to derive a greater sense of achievement.

Age 50–80 years

This is the very interesting phase of life. You will have paid off your mortgage, maybe have moved to a better house, suburb, country, or town. You would have been setting aside money for your retirement, accumulating superannuation, and attracting assets either as additional property or investments in shares. Your children would have finished their educational requirements and now will be responsible for their own lives and lifestyle. Now you will have freedom to do as and when you want and like. Make sure you enjoy it!

3 Commitment

The word commitment is, according to the dictionary that I have at hand, the word for dedication to a cause or a policy and also a pledge or an undertaking. It is also an engagement or obligation that restricts the freedom of action.

So how does this word, commitment, play a part in your life?

Once you have decided on a course of action, let's use the example of the finalising of your twelve years of attending school. We are not referring to the courses that you are involved with, just the action of finishing school and graduating.

The commitment component is the action of attending school on a daily basis and undertaking the activity that you are instructed to do by your teacher. Or it may relate to the part that you play in the cricket team, where you are expected to train twice a week and play once a week. It is attending to these requirements which are satisfying your commitment to fulfil the needs of yourself, team members, school students, family members, and district occupants.

So what would happen if you did not commit to a course or an action? Nothing. Nothing at all. You would wander through life with no ambition, no sense of achievement, no sense of fulfilment. You would probably stumble through life and, furthermore, may never achieve anything by which your personal success could be measured and of which you would be proud. What do you think is imperative to your future?

By committing to a course of action, you can gauge the steps and stages you must complete to finalise the commitment process and create the sense of achievement.

So then, having achieved success in your chosen field, it will spur you onto other areas in your life in which you can commit, follow through, and gain that wonderful sense of achievement.

Some Questions to Define What the Future May Look Like

Now stepping back in time.

Think back to where you were when you were around 5–7 years of age.

What were you interested in? What are your innate skills, the things that you derived much satisfaction from completing?

So what am I saying?

To give you an example of what I am asking, we will discuss young Jimmy. You will read a lot of Jimmy and his achievements in the following chapters. Jimmy is not his real name but the achievements that he has enjoyed are all true and correct.

When Jimmy was around the age of 5–6 years of age, he started to grow chilli bushes from seed. He experimented with different soils, different amounts of water, different manures and plant foods, and different locations in the garden, either being windy or sunny or shady. The plants grew, and Jimmy's sense of achievement derived from the commitment that he had undertaken was realised.

Of course, Jimmy's parents looked in on what he was doing, asking appropriate questions, and just keeping a quiet eye on the activities.

So do you think that the interest in growing the chilli bushes had a bearing on Jimmy's final occupation?

No, it didn't, but the attitude that he developed by committing to an activity and seeing that activity through to its completion, even though he ultimately gave away the chilli bushes that he had grown to friends, family, and neighbours, gave him a sense of success and which he found to be very inspiring.

If he had not maintained his commitment to the chilli bushes, they would have withered and died. Your goals (dreams) are your chilli bushes and they need to be nurtured.

Maybe you do not actually want to grow chilli bushes, and I don't blame you. But this was just one of many things that cost very little but by which Jimmy experienced the sense of success.

So in an effort to know and understand what your innate skills are, you need to undertake a SWOT analysis as shown in chapter 1, The Starting Block. In responding to the questions asked, take your time, spend some time thinking about your life, what you have undertaken in your life, what you have achieved so far in your life. From that, you should draw information which will assist in your responses to the questions posed. The final question is about threats. This does not infer that there will be a terrible future waiting for you. Rather the question asks what hurdles are there for you to jump. A threat can be just an obstacle that needs to be conquered, or it requires a closer look at the commitment that you have elected. A refinement of that commitment to make it more targeted to an area, rather than being wider with less opportunity for you, may be required for you to be able to be successful.

5 A Little Bit of Explanation

I have written this book in the hope that it will assist people to be in a position to evaluate the needs of various occupations and to place themselves in a position of success, gaining respect and enjoyment from their daily work activities.

In school, when a teacher or a careers advisor stands and teaches about occupations, it is in a very wide, non specific manner, rarely targeting an actual occupation from the beginning to the end, warts and all. Neither is this book able to identify each and every nook and cranny of each and every occupation.

If you start your working life as a school teacher, you may change after a period of time, let's suggest ten years or so, and you may go and write text books on other subjects in a different manner, which you feel would be a preferable manner for students – allowing for a greater insight, which you have gained by your experience on a particular subject to be revealed.

What Career Should I Choose?

You may have completed your studies in a field of engineering and then progress on to becoming an inventor.

There are many, many examples of career movements once you have finalised your studies, but which allow you to be more involved in the outcome of an activity. It may just be as simple as completing a Masters in your chosen field.

One area that you can access to be aware of what jobs, occupations, or careers are available is the TISC book, (refer to *www.tisc.edu.au*, for more information or go to your local news agency as they normally stock the publication). This publication identifies the needs and the prerequisites required for a particular field of endeavour, and the areas of study required together with the Institutes which offer the required study courses. The component that this publication does not cover is the income that can be derived from that occupation. The income relative to each occupation does rely upon the level and depth of skills gained in the course of gaining the skills. You can read in the position vacant posting, the various wages or salaries available for different positions in a newspaper or on the internet, try a site such as Seek.com.

The last area that I will discuss here is the need for you to be very aware of your own skills – the skills that you have developed throughout your life just by being yourself. An example is you may excel at playing Soccer; you may be able to become a professional soccer player as a result of the efforts you have made as you rose through the ranks as a soccer player and the skills that you have attained as a result. Then again, you may see success in becoming a soccer coach, and the effort and rewards that may result along the way, or as a manufacturer of football boots, allowing for greater comfort to be enjoyed by all football players. On the other hand, you may wish to be a designer and manufacturer of football jerseys. As you can see, every field of endeavour has many fields within it. The trick is to find the one that you would enjoy the most.

The purpose of this book is to identify where the opportunities can be found, upon completing the attached workbook.

Questions About Yourself

Now let's get started, getting down to what needs to be done, how, why, when, and where.

The very first thing that is required is to identify where you *do not* want to work.

This should create a rather long list, but it is important as a tool to use. Whilst we always aim for Yes, and never a No, this process easily allows us to identify the No's in our lives.

An example: I do not want to work in a pig farm or a chook farm. So from the list of occupations, you can delete these occupations and any akin to them.

Of course, the other side of the coin is that now you have imposed the need to gather skills that will allow you to work in an area that has a prerequisite of qualifications of one type or another. Then you must be able to gain the required qualifications.

Having a qualification does not mean nor indicate that you have attended university or a TAFE college. But is simply the result of having passed an exam. So, once more, the reward is in passing an exam in a discipline or a vocation that allows you to trade in any occupation, be it an electrician or a plumber or a doctor or an accountant, to name but a few occupations out of many that are available.

Of course, once you have gained the qualification in a discipline, there is nothing stopping you from then moving into a different field of endeavour.

Once you have passed the all important final examination then it is wise to commence working for someone who has a long history of working in that field of endeavour. Then you will have successfully moved from the theory taught in the classroom to the practical application that you now have the opportunity of. Such as a doctor who completes an internship by which he receives supervised training in a hospital, acting as an assistant to a doctor or a physician or a surgeon.

So now that you have clarified what it is that you do *not* want to do, it is time to think about you identify what it is you do want to do!

How Do You Do This?

7 What Are Your Likes and Dislikes?

Create a list, which, in part, could be as simple as the following:

1. I do not want to work outside;
2. I do not want to work above floor level; you may be frightened of heights;
3. I do not want to work with children;
4. I do not want to work in a nursing home for the elderly;
5. I do not want to work in a noisy area;
6. I want to work in the same location all the time;
7. I welcome travel, either intrastate or interstate or even overseas;
8. I like wearing a uniform;
9. I like dealing with the public;
10. I faint when I see blood;

And so the process continues.

By responding to each and every point listed here, you are narrowing the list of occupations that you would enjoy.

By narrowing the list, some occupations with similar traits should start to become apparent.

Back to discussions about young Jimmy – when he and I worked through the list, and we only had the TISC booklet to guide us, the component or the part that took us the longest was the process of knowing what he did want to do versus what he would never ever want to do. So he listed those skills and talents that he saw as being enjoyable, and of course, the ones he saw as being not enjoyable at all.

By pursuing this path, it will, eventually, lead to shortening the occupations available for you to pursue and that is just the outcome that is required.

# What Would You Like to Achieve?

What a difficult question!

Where does it start, and where does it end?

Does it relate to the income generated by your occupation?

Well, the answer to that is no: the question actually related to what would make you happy?

Happy as in what would you like to do as an occupation or career?

Follow through the steps within the four-step schedule, allowing for plenty of time. You, for the major part, will have to review all the nooks and crannies of your mind, and your memory, to be in the best position to evaluate and correctly answer the questions posed within the workbook.

Identifying what occupation best suits you is but part of the steps and stages of your life as has been identified in Chapter 2. As you glide through the stages of your life, major points stand out but for the main part, life becomes a bank of memories, and the devil is in the detail of them.

The occupation that you choose, and work hard to attain, should also give you definable benefits.

Those benefits are things like paid holiday time, paid sick leave, and regular income. The better the choice of occupation, the better the level of income you can expect to receive. The more time spent on educating yourself, the better financial reward should be available to you.

Some people start work at the age of fifteen, part-time in a takeaway food shop as kitchen hand or selling the product at the front counter. This is usually just to make money, so that they can start to be independent of their parents and to enable them to buy all the toys that they require at their stage in life. I mean, how can you live without then latest and greatest gadgets?

But, it is doing this job and attending to the requirements that their employment contract dictates, that is part of the maturing process. Some people commence at a food takeaway store, and become so involved that they, in time, become an integral part of the business management team.

Others gain jobs to pay their way whilst they study to achieve their occupational requirements. So now for an update on Jimmy – yes, Jimmy worked his way through the TISC booklet, and, after much toing and froing whilst measuring his likes and dislikes, the decision was made that Jimmy would become either a geophysicist or a geologist and then maybe a surveyor.

Bearing in mind that, at this time, Jimmy was approximately sixteen years of age, the decision had taken many hours of discussion, much soul searching, not to mention the diligent attitude that he had adopted. He was very keen to know what lay ahead of him at the end of his formal education.

So armed with the facts and the various occupations that are listed above, Jimmy then had to make a decision as to whether he was inclined to attend university or attend the school of surveying. As life does at times, it threw a large curve ball towards Jimmy. He was in year eleven, studying diligently, working his way through five *tee* subjects. Happy with what he was doing. Jimmy also maintained an interest in playing golf and was a member of the local junior golf squad that played at various sites over the metropolitan area. Jimmy managed to play golf off a handicap of, from memory, eight at that time. Jimmy had won the president's trophy at the local privately owned golf club, the year before, when he was fifteen years of age.

So what was the curve ball sent Jimmy's way?

He sat his mock *tee* exams, he attended to everything within his power to ensure that he was open, honest, accurate, and correct as is his nature, then his exam papers were marked by the teacher, who failed Jimmy in two subjects. A major drama followed, with discussions, and then Jimmy's purposeful resolution to discover where he had made errors in those two exam papers. The end of the story is that the teacher had incorrectly marked both of the papers, and Jimmy would have passed them if the error had not occurred.

Back to square one, you would have thought but no – a fair bit of discussion followed in the ensuing weeks between Jimmy and his parents. The decision was made, that Jimmy would graduate from high school, not bother about attending university but rather attend the school of surveying. He applied to be admitted as a student and, after being interviewed by the department head, was admitted.

The next step was for Jimmy to get a job. The job needed to be on the weekends so that he could attend school, it needed to pay enough to cover his education costs, (his food and living costs were still being paid, willingly, by his parents). The local industrial hire shop was looking for staff and hired Jimmy. Jimmy excelled at the shop, he hired equipment out, he took the returned equipment, he maintained equipment, using the knowledge that he gained from attending to his surveying course. All in all, he enjoyed the job and the manner that he was treated by the owners. By the way, so impressed were they with Jimmy that now some eight years later, he still hires equipment for his own use, free of charge.

So now, what is Jimmy up to? A very good question. He has completed his diploma in surveying and his advanced diploma in surveying and has been working for a civil engineering company for the past seven years.

The lesson from Jimmy's achievements is not to know what Jimmy did, but more to the point, how he did it – one step at a time. He never lost sight of his own life, sporting ambitions, social engagements, but he had the commitment to succeed in his chosen field, to make the best of the opportunity, to study as much as he deemed to be required to be in a position to earn good money. For Jimmy, once his income had passed the $100,000 gross, at the age of twenty-seven, he was happy.

So now that you have diligently read through these pages, hopefully you are feeling inspired enough to follow through the last chapter of this book and then complete the four-step schedule so that you may also be able to achieve a sense of fulfilment gained from being successful with a commitment.

9 When Do You Think You Will Retire?

What a strange question, especially when you have only just got your foot on the accelerator pedal of your working life?

When you commence something as big as the journey of your working life, then you must admit to yourself that at some point in time, there will be an end or a conclusion to it. I have covered this topic in Chapter 2, included it in the stages of life section.

Back to the discussion – you have read every page of this book and are sitting poised to proceed to the four-step schedule.

Stop right there! Once you are in a position to evaluate an occupation that seems to fit the niche requirement that you have identified, then you have proceeded to ensure that it is financially rewarding enough to keep you fed and clothed. Now I am asking you to consider when you expect to retire from the workforce. Granted, commonly accepted retirement age is sixty-five years old, but I know many a person who is still working fulltime at seventy years of age.

What Career Should I Choose?

Do they still want to work, or is it just a habit and a routine that they fear changing? When you get to the age of sixty-five, I am sure that you would like to be in the position to retire from your normal work day habits, but perhaps still work but in a different manner.

The age at which you will retire will be a direct result of the income derived from your occupation, and how much of that income has been set to work on its own, for example, the buying of shares or real estate rental properties or stamp collecting. This is not my area of expertise and so it is not up to me to give you a finite plan, just to mention that this occupation that you have selected must do a lot more than just feed and clothe you as it must see to your future, indeed all your needs for all your days on this earth.

PART 2
The Four-step Schedule

Here we are ready to start the four-step schedule. You have just read, on almost every page, the importance of completing the schedule but let me reiterate.

To be able to assess where your future is, is almost a journey of self-discovery. One that relies upon open and honest answers from yourself, even if you get up and walk away from it, leaving it be for a day or two, then returning, reinvigorated, ready to attend to your commitment of completing your four-step schedule.

This is your book, it belongs only to you. If you make a mistake, erase errors or score them through with a pen, it is your option to do so. In my mind, make as many mistakes as possible, in doing so, you are solidifying the thought patterns required to complete this workbook, and therefore, strengthening your commitment.

The four-step schedule starts on the next page. There are three identical four-step schedules, complete the first in the next month or so. Set the book aside, leaving it for another six months or so, then complete the second four-step schedule. Once you have finished that, review your responses compared with the initial response that you had, in the first four-step schedule. Then, once more, set the book aside for a period of twelve months, then complete the third four-step schedule. Once all the questions have been answered, review each against the responses in the previous two.

What has changed? Is it a result of the personal growth you are enjoying derived from reading this book and from having completed the four-step schedules?

So now, over the page to commence your journey.

WHAT CAREER SHOULD I CHOOSE?

The Four-step Schedule A

Today's date _____

Respond to each question:

Swot Analysis

What are your strengths?

_____
_____
_____
_____
_____
_____
_____
_____
_____
_____
_____
_____
_____
_____
_____

What are your weaknesses?

What Career Should I Choose?

What are your opportunities?

What are your threats or obstacles?

What Career Should I Choose?

What are your dislikes? What are your likes?

Rabbit

What are your hobbies?

What Career Should I Choose?

Write a list of occupations that you now find interesting:

RABBIT

Write a list of required activity to achieve that occupation:

What Career Should I Choose?

The Four-step Schedule B

Today's date _____

Respond to each question:

Swot Analysis

What are your strengths?

_____
_____
_____
_____
_____
_____
_____
_____
_____
_____
_____
_____
_____
_____
_____

What Career Should I Choose?

What are your weaknesses?

What are your opportunities?

What Career Should I Choose?

What are your threats or obstacles?

Rabbit

What are your dislikes? What are your likes?

What Career Should I Choose?

What are your hobbies?

Rabbit

Write a list of occupations that you now find interesting:

What Career Should I Choose?

Write a list of required activity to achieve that occupation:

Rabbit

The Four-step Schedule C

Today's date _____

Respond to each question:

Swot Analysis

What are your strengths?

_____
_____
_____
_____
_____
_____
_____
_____
_____
_____
_____
_____
_____
_____
_____
_____
_____

What are your weaknesses?

What Career Should I Choose?

_____
_____
_____
_____
_____
_____
_____
_____
_____
_____
_____

What are your opportunities?

_____
_____
_____
_____
_____
_____
_____
_____
_____
_____
_____
_____

Rabbit

What are your threats?

What Career Should I Choose?

What are your dislikes? What are your likes?

What are your hobbies?

What Career Should I Choose?

Write a list of occupations that you now find interesting:

Rabbit

Write a list of required activity to achieve that occupation:

What Career Should I Choose?

Now that you have completed all three four-step schedules, it is time to evaluate your discoveries.

Whilst attending to the completion of the SWOT analysis, what has changed?

1. Have you found out how strong you are, physically or mentally?
2. Have you eliminated your weaknesses from an occupational choice?
3. Have you risen to the challenge of an opportunity?
4. Have you challenged your threats?

In the evaluation of your dislikes and your likes, which area is stronger for the likes? And will it lead to an occupation?

Will it be a skill developed to become a saleable skill?

Is it short term or long term?

Now I assume that you have reviewed the web site of the TISC booklet, and by now, I expect that you have devoured the contents of that booklet.

So what have you discovered, is it that your studies have not been on quite the right path? This is a frequent discovery!

In finding that, have you also found how to remedy the problem of incorrect studies. If you live in Western Australia, I would guide you in

What Career Should I Choose?

the direction of Tuart Hill College, to name but one, there are many places for adult education throughout the world, look them up in your local telephone directory.

Once more, and again I reiterate, find a job that keeps life and soul together until you have achieved your ultimate goal. Yes, I agree it sounds a lot easier than it is to do, but one year of your life is and as such is a small amount of time in the overall scheme of things.

Now that you have done all that has been asked of you throughout this book, it is time to put theory into practice if you haven't so far.

Do the study:

Resolve any issues about your life and the achievements that you are committed to:

If you have issues that remain unsolved ask someone, like me. You can email for support, at any point in time. So email me at

....

....

I would also appreciate some feedback.

How have you found this book?

Do you have any suggestions to be included in a revised version?

In conclusion, if you have found the theory to be very interesting and stimulating but are more than as little daunted by attending to Part 2 – The four-step schedule, I can offer a one-to-one tutorial to assist you in your endeavours.

Visit my website:
www.whatcareershouldichoosebyRABBIT.com